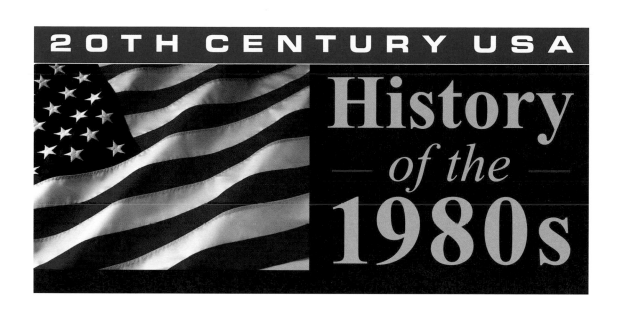

20TH CENTURY USA

History of the 1980s

Rennay Craats

WEIGL PUBLISHERS INC.

Published by Weigl Publishers Inc.
123 South Broad Street, Box 227
Mankato, MN, USA
Web site: http://www.weigl.com

Library of Congress Cataloging-in-Publication Data available upon request
from the publisher. Fax (507) 388-2746 for the attention of the Publishing
Records Department.

ISBN 1-930954-39-5

Printed and bound in the United States of America
1 2 3 4 5 6 7 8 9 0   05 04 03 02 01

Senior Editor
Jared Keen

Series Editor
Carlotta Lemeiux

Copy Editor
Heather Kissock

Layout and Design
Warren Clark
Carla Pelky

Photo Research
Joe Nelson

Photograph Credits

Alberta Archives: page 39T; Archive Photos: pages 23, 25, 28, 43; Bettmann/CORBIS:
pages 29, 30, 34; CORBIS: page 42; Digital Vision Ltd: page 32B; Frank Edwards/Fotos
International/Archive Photos: page 40; Express Newspapers/Archive Photos: page 20, 31; Frank
Flavin: page 9; Kristen Higgens: pages 14M, 15; Peter Keegan/Archive Photos: page 33; Bob
Krist/CORBIS: page 12B; NASA: pages 3B, 7B, 8, 26L, 26R, 27M; Sorcha McGinnes: page
36MR; Photofest: pages 3TL, 10T, 11, 12T, 13, 14T, 16T, 36T, 37M, 38T, 41; © Neal
Preston/CORBIS: pages 6L, 10B; Reuters/Pat Benic/Archive Photos: page 18; Reuters/John
Gibbons/Archive Photos: page 38B; Reuters/Stringer/Archive Photos: page 19B; Reuters/Arthur
Tsang/Archive Photos: pages 7BR, 17; SAGA/Frank Capri/Archive Photos: page 24; Joseph
Sohm; ChromoSohm Inc./CORBIS: pages 3TR, 39B; Jim Sugar Photography/CORBIS: page
35; Gary Trotter; Eye Ubiquitous/CORBIS: page 22; University of Utah: page 27TR; U.S.
Department of Energy: page 16B; Vietnam Veterans Memorial Fund: pages 6R, 32T; White
House/Archive Photos: page 21.

Every reasonable effort has been made to trace ownership and to obtain permission to reprint
copyright material. The publishers would be pleased to have any errors or omissions brought to
their attention so that they may be corrected in subsequent printings.

USA 1980s Contents

Entertainment 10

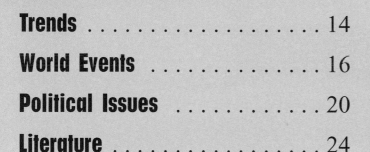

Science & Technology 26

Immigration 38

Berlin Wall Falls

President Shot

Chernobyl Disaster

AMERICA

Terrorist Attack

Famine in Africa

A Ride in Space

Deadly Earthquake

E.T. Captures Hearts

Carl Lewis Races for Gold

People learn about what is happening across this vast country through newspapers, television, and radio programs. The events reach much farther than the areas in which they unfold—the history they create writes the story of a nation.

20th Century USA: History of the 1980s presents a brief look at the who, what, where, when, why, and how that lay behind the important headlines. This book explores the key people and events that helped shape this fascinating decade.

Many of the stories in this book made an incredible impact on the population and have since become part of the American identity. The *Challenger* explosion shocked the country and made people think seriously about the space program. The stock market crash changed lives, shook the economy, and brought an end to the "greed" era. Americans cheered Olympic athletes Carl Lewis and Florence Griffith Joyner on to gold medals.

AIDS Identified

Woman Benched

Austrian Terminates

Preppie Power

Royal Wedding

Smuggling People

Islanders on Top

Black Monday

Live Aid

There were also several amazing events that happened outside the U.S. They affected Americans just the same. People worldwide rallied together to help ease the famine in Africa. The fall of the Berlin Wall gave people hope. These events are forever etched in the memories of Americans.

The stories covered in these pages are only a few of many events that occurred in the 1980s. There are a lot of ways to find out more about this fascinating decade. The Internet and libraries are great places to learn more about the sports, music, politics, economy, and trends of the eighties. There are stacks of

old 1980s publications saved on microfilm for you to dive into.

History is not just what happened a hundred years ago. History is made each day by celebrities and everyday people like yourselves. Turn the page and discover the people and places that made headlines in this eventful decade, the 1980s.

USA 1980s Time Line

1980

Miami becomes the new home of thousands of Cuban immigrants. See page 38 for more information on Fidel Castro's plan.

1980

Mount Saint Helens starts to rumble in Washington. Discover what happened next on page 9.

1980

No stars and stripes fly at the 1980 Olympic Games. Find out why on page 28.

1980

An actor enters the White House. See what Ronald Reagan brought to America on page 20.

1981

Music fans welcome music videos twenty-four hours a day in 1981. Learn more about MTV on page 10.

1981

Peanuts and popcorn sales drop dramatically. With baseball players on strike, fans are left without their boys of summer. Turn to page 29 to find out why the players walked off the field and when they came back.

1981

Typewriters become a thing of the past when IBM introduces the personal computer. To learn more about the success of this new technology, turn to page 26.

1982

Women fail to achieve equality in the Constitution. To read more about the defeat of the Equal Rights Amendment, see page 33.

1982

A new disease terrifies people around the world. Find out about the discovery of AIDS on page 27.

1982

After years of debate, the Vietnam Memorial is dedicated in Washington, D.C. To read about this controversial memorial, turn to page 32.

1983

The nation says a tearful goodbye to a wacky group of medics when *M*A*S*H* airs its final episode. To learn more about this hit comedy, turn to page 13.

1983

The New York Islanders win their fourth Stanley Cup. Discover more about this dream team on page 30.

MTV cast

Vietnam Memorial

1984

The USSR responds to the **boycott** of the 1980 Moscow Olympics by boycotting the Summer Olympics in Los Angeles. Turn to page 28 to find out more.

1984

A poisonous gas leak at a Union Carbide plant in Bhopal, India, kills and injures many people. Learn how this accident happened on page 18.

1985

Millions of people pull out their checkbooks as they tune into a televised international benefit concert. To find out how Live Aid helped African famine victims, see page 41.

1985

The Soviet Union has a new leader. He is going to change the country. Turn to page 19 to learn what made Mikhail Gorbachev so important.

1986

An explosion and fire blast through a nuclear power plant in the Soviet Union. The far-reaching effects of the Chernobyl accident are detailed on page 16.

1986

A burst of fire takes over the sky. The space shuttle Challenger explodes, killing its crew. Turn to page 8 to find out how this disaster happened.

1987

Black Monday brings the stock market crashing down. Learn what resulted from this economic disaster on page 34.

1988

A cease-fire ends the Iran-Iraq War. To find out how this war started and how long it lasted, see page 19.

1988

Republican George Bush beats Democrat Michael Dukakis in the presidential election. Turn to page 23 to read about the new leader.

1988

Salman Rushdie's new novel hits bookstores. Turn to page 25 to find out how his words could be the death of him.

1989

The Berlin Wall comes crashing down. East and West Germans are thrilled to cross the border. Page 18 has more details.

1989

A Chinese clash in Tiananmen Square is watched by millions of people on television. Find out why the army opened fire on protesters on page 17.

1989

Baseball hero Pete Rose falls from grace. Read more about why this legend will never be in the Hall of Fame on page 31.

Challenger explodes

Tiananmen Square

Challenger Explosion

On January 28, 1986, millions of people watched as NASA's *Challenger* space shuttle was launched. Seconds later, the sky was filled with fire and debris. The shuttle had exploded. It was the worst accident in the space program's history. All seven crew members died. Among them was high school teacher Christa McAuliffe. She was the first private citizen to be sent into space. President Reagan immediately set up a commission to investigate the cause of the explosion. Investigators discovered that it had been caused by faulty rocket seals. Hot gases had seeped out and set the shuttle's fuel on fire. The country was shocked that such a disaster could happen, and the explosion put some of NASA's plans on hold. The seven space travelers were honored as heroes.

"We will never forget them nor the last time we saw them this morning as they prepared for their journey and waved goodbye and slipped the surly bonds of Earth to touch the face of God."

Ronald Reagan

■ *Challenger* explodes, claiming the lives of all seven on board.

Terrorists Attack Pan Am Flight

On December 21, 1988, families and friends eagerly awaited the arrival of Pan Am flight 103. It never reached its New York destination. The plane was cruising at 31,000 feet when it exploded over Lockerbie, Scotland. All 259 people on board, including thirty-six Syracuse University students and several members of the U.S. military, were killed. Eleven more on the ground were killed as the plane crashed into rows of houses.

Investigators discovered that a bomb had caused the disaster.

"I was driving past the filling station when the aircraft crashed. The whole sky lit up, and the sky was actually raining fire. It was just like liquid."

A witness to the crash

The explosives had been planted in the luggage area of the plane. Authorities believed Libyan terrorists were responsible for the attack. Two baggage handlers thought to be Libyan secret agents were accused. Libya would not release the men for trial. The United Nations declared **sanctions** against Libya and blocked access to its foreign assets. It took more than ten years for the accused bombers to face charges in court.

Mount Saint Helens Erupts

Mount Saint Helens had been quiet since 1857, but it started sending out warnings early in 1980. The volcano began to rumble and spit out ash and small boulders. Residents were told to leave the area, while geologists kept an eye on it. Mount Saint Helens finally erupted on May 18.

The eruption was violent, blowing off the volcano's top and spewing out fiery lava. Ash was sent 60,000 feet into the air. The mountain shrank from being 9,677 feet high to 8,365 feet high after the eruption. Clouds of ash settled for hundreds of miles around. The blast caused earthquakes, fires, floods, and mudslides. The area's animal and plant life were seriously damaged. About sixty people were killed, and the eruption caused $2.7 billion in damages. It was the first eruption in the continental U.S. in more than sixty years and one of the most violent eruptions ever.

DEADLY EARTHQUAKE

On October 17, 1989, many San Franciscans were driving home to watch the World Series championships. Then the ground started to rumble. At 5:06 PM, the area experienced one of the most destructive earthquakes in California's history. It measured 7.1 on the Richter scale. San Francisco's most destructive earthquake had occurred in 1906. It registered 7.8 and killed hundreds of residents. Around ninety people were killed in the 1989 quake, as highways and bridges collapsed around them. The earthquake caused $6 billion in damages during the fifteen seconds it lasted. Newer buildings had been constructed to survive earthquakes, but many of the older ones crumbled. However, it did not take long for the city to rebuild and move on.

Exxon Valdez Oil Spill

On March 24, 1989, an Exxon oil tanker hit a reef off the coast of Prince William Sound. The collision opened up the tanker, and 11 million gallons of oil spilled into the sea. Crews managed to move only 1 million gallons of oil from the *Valdez* into another tanker. It was one of the biggest spills in U.S. history. It was also one of the most harmful.

Volunteers tried to clean up the oil before it destroyed plants and wildlife, but there was not much they could do.

Hundreds of thousands of animals died as a result of the Exxon *Valdez* oil spill.

The oil in the water and on the shore killed many animals, including 580,000 birds and 5,500 otters. Heavy with oil on their feathers and skin, some drowned. Others froze to death. Still others ate plants that were coated with oil. Rescuers saved some animals that became caught in the spill, but most of the victims died.

Exxon paid more than $2 billion for the clean-up and $100 million in fines. This is the most ever paid for an environmental crime. The company paid another $900 million in lawsuits, along with $5 billion in damages to the Alaskan fishers. Scientists are still trying to restore the **ecological** balance in the area.

I Want My MTV

In 1981, a new television station, called MTV (Music Television), was launched by Warner Amex Satellite Entertainment Company. Americans could now watch music videos and programming twenty-four-hours-a-day. MTV played concerts, videos, and interviews of the hottest people in music. The station quickly attracted 2.5 million subscribers in forty-eight states. The subscription base tripled in only one year. The station brought stars from all over the world into America's living rooms. This meant a great deal to the stars, too. Exposure on the station often meant a jump in record sales of between 15 and 20 percent. Just by appearing on MTV, some musicians became superstars before they had even played in front of a live audience.

 Alan Hunter, Martha Quinn, John Goodman, Nina Blackwood, and J. J. Jackson were the first video jockeys on MTV. Now MTV can be seen around the world.

The Brat Pack

A group of young, successful actors made headlines in the 1980s. These stars included Demi Moore, Judd Nelson, Molly Ringwald, Ally Sheedy, Emilio Estevez, and Rob Lowe. Their movies, such as *The Breakfast Club, St. Elmo's Fire, Pretty in Pink,* and *Sixteen Candles,* were smash hits. These actors worked together and played together, too. They soon became symbols of the 1980s.

A magazine writer called the group the "Brat Pack." The name stuck. It labeled the

■ One of the most popular Brat Pack movies, *The Breakfast Club*, was a smash hit.

actors as wild, spoiled kids. As the eighties drew to a close, the Brat Packers lost their appeal with audiences. A more conservative lifestyle was encouraged, and the Brat Pack no longer represented public views. This shift made it difficult for many of these stars to land good roles. They stopped making movies and hanging out together. They hoped this would help them to be taken seriously. A few of the Brat Packers remained successful. Most of them worked for many years to get rid of the "Brat Pack" label.

FRAMING ROGER RABBIT

■ Steven Spielberg's movie *Who Framed Roger Rabbit?* was an instant hit when it was released in 1988. The actors and animated characters on the screen spent the movie trying to figure out who the real murderer was—everyone knew the bumbling Roger could never kill anyone. Audiences followed Detective Eddie Valiant, played by Bob Hoskins, as he tried to prove a 'toon's innocence. Spielberg's combination of animation and live action kept audiences spellbound. Roger Rabbit won Academy Awards for sound effects, visual effects, and film editing. It also won a special award for animation direction because of the way it brought people and cartoons together.

The movie was a success with both children and adults alike. It is entertaining and witty enough for adults to enjoy and easy for children to understand.

Lost Ark Raided

Indiana Jones was more than an archeology professor. He was an action hero who, starting in 1981, thrilled audiences with his adventures. *Raiders of the Lost Ark*, starring Harrison Ford, was a block office hit. Indy does it all in the Indiana Jones movies—he barely escapes a rolling boulder, battles a pit full of snakes, is tempted by evil ghosts, is chased by tanks, and has to find his way out of a booby-trapped tomb. Americans loved the fun and thrills of these movies. They also loved Harrison Ford, who became a Hollywood superstar. *Raiders* was the first movie of its kind, yet it brought old movie **serials** back to life. *Indiana Jones and the Temple of Doom* and *Indiana Jones and the Last Crusade* followed shortly after. The Indiana Jones movies continue to enjoy success in video form.

E.T. Captures Hearts

In 1982, a creature from outer space invaded the hearts of Americans. Steven Spielberg's blockbuster tear-jerker *E.T. The Extraterrestrial* is the story of an odd little being who is accidentally left on Earth by his fellow travelers. E.T. finds help and love in a young boy named Elliott and his family. He also finds a way to "phone home." In the process, he brings the family together.

In the beginning, executives at Columbia studios were offered the story but turned it down. They did not think movie-watchers would enjoy it. They were wrong. *E.T. The Extraterrestrial* won Academy Awards for music, sound, sound effects, and visual effects. It also made more money than any other movie in history. More than that, *E.T.* made Spielberg known for more than robots and action movies. He proved he could be successful with a "people-centered" movie.

■ *E.T.* brought joy to the hearts of children and adults. It is still one of the most popular movies of all time.

BACK TO THE FUTURE

■ In 1985, Michael J. Fox took Americans on a trip back to the 1950s in *Back to the Future*. Fox's character, Marty McFly, has to make sure he does not change history. His mother, played by Lea Thompson, develops a crush on Marty, and he has to try to find a way to get his parents together. With help from Christopher Lloyd, who plays a crazy time machine inventor, McFly patches up his parents' teenage relationship and then returns to the eighties. The movie was a great success with audiences. It won an Academy Award for Best Sound Effects. Americans loved the idea so much that sequels were released in 1989 and again in 1990.

Family Values

Television in the 1980s reflected many different kinds of families. *The Cosby Show* aired in 1984. It presented a close-knit, upper-middle-class family led by Bill Cosby, who played a doctor. Cosby also created the program and worked hard to break many of the stereotypes that people had about African-Americans. The characters on the show encounter minor problems that are resolved with love and laughs within a thirty-minute program. The sitcom hit number one in 1985 and stayed on top for five

■ *The Cosby Show* was a popular family-oriented comedy.

seasons, until it was bumped out of the number one position by a very different family show.

Roseanne, starring Roseanne Barr, took a sarcastic look at blue-collar life in small-town America. *Roseanne* was launched in 1988, and audiences loved it. They appreciated its honesty. Life did have real problems, and sometimes it was tough to make ends meet. Many people struggling to pay the bills and keep strong relationships within their families could relate to *Roseanne*. The comedy stayed high in the ratings until it went off the air in 1997.

Night-and-Day News

In June 1980, businessman Ted Turner launched a twenty-four-hour-a-day news station. Cable News Network (CNN) was the first station in the world to focus only on news. CNN started when Turner bought a local Atlanta station that was in trouble. He used this station to send broadcasts from coast to coast. During CNN's first year, it aired live coverage of the presidential conventions and election campaigns. Over time, CNN has broadcast important events, including courtroom cases and NASA space missions. The station had a small budget—only $30 billion—and some people

■ CNN has grown into a huge news distributor. It has channels all over the world, from the Middle East to Vietnam.

thought it would not last, but it proved the skeptics wrong. CNN provided high-quality news broadcasts for the growing number of Americans who wanted to be informed.

By the mid-1990s, CNN had accumulated 62 million subscribers in the U.S. and 67 million more throughout the world.

A Sad Goodbye to M*A*S*H

After a rocky first year, network executives decided to take a chance and renew *M*A*S*H*. They never regretted their decision. The show caught on with audiences across the country. For eleven years, television audiences shared their Monday nights with smart aleck Hawkeye Pierce, nutty Max Klinger, Radar O'Reilly and his teddy bear, and the rest of the doctors and nurses at U.S. Army hospital No. 4077. Actors including Alan Alda as Hawkeye, Loretta Swit as Margaret "Hot Lips" Houlihan, and McLean Stevenson as Colonel Blake, drew loyal fans to the show. The half-hour comedy made people laugh, but it also addressed serious issues. The series followed the sarcastic, funny, and at times bitter characters through their experiences in the Korean War. At the end of the run, the networks aired a two-and-a-half-hour farewell show on February 28, 1983. *M*A*S*H* fans cried as the members of their favorite television war family went their separate ways. A record 125 million people watched the last episode. *M*A*S*H* won thirteen major Emmy awards, many of which went to Alan Alda for writing, acting, and directing.

HOME ARCADES

■ In the early 1980s, home video games were out. Instead, Americans rushed to plug quarters into the newest games at the arcades. Pac-Man was a favorite—a yellow, button-shaped creature that raced around a maze eating dots while being chased by ghosts. The barrel-hopping gorilla in Donkey Kong and the road-crossing amphibian in Frogger were also very popular. By the mid-1980s, computer companies, including Atari, Colecovision, and Nintendo, began producing home versions of the popular games. These games had more advanced graphics than earlier home games. Players' interest returned to home systems. Americans no longer had to go to the arcades. The arcades came home to them on their own televisions.

Austrian Terminates

Arnold Schwarzenegger swapped bodybuilding for Hollywood blockbusters. In 1982, the former Mr. Universe starred in *Conan the Barbarian*. Then, in 1984, he played the lead in its sequel, *Conan the Destroyer*. Each of the movies made more than $100 million and made the Austrian a wanted man in action movies. In 1984, he also starred in James Cameron's *Terminator*. Schwarzenegger plays a cyborg assassin from the future, who was sent back to the eighties to kill a woman whose son would become a threat twenty years down the road. He fails in his attempt, but comes back as the child's protector in *Terminator 2: Judgement Day* in 1991.

■ The Terminator's imposing physique struck fear into the hearts of moviegoers.

No More Vinyl

In 1982, U.S. music lovers were introduced to a new, high-tech way of listening to albums. Cassette tapes and vinyl records were out. Compact disks were the way of the future. Americans were excited by the state-of-the-art CD. Phillips Corporation and Sony released their new lightweight disks, which promised the highest-quality recordings. The disks

■ Compact disk technology is still popular today and has paved the way for Mini Disks and Digital Video Disks.

were very small, measuring 4 3/4 inches across rather than the 12 inches of albums. Music was recorded on each metallic pit on the disk. A CD player used a laser to read these pits and convert them into sound. Using a laser decreased wear on the disk, which made it last longer. CDs also held more information, or music, than a cassette or album could. They became popular and quickly took over the music market from vinyl records.

Americans Scramble to Adopt

The adoption rate hit the roof in 1983. Young Americans gladly promised to give their Cabbage Patch Kids a good home. Each doll was a little different from the others and came with its own adoption certificate. Its owner became its adoptive parent. But getting these dolls home in the

■ Each Cabbage Patch Kid came to its new "parent" with an original name.

first place was not always easy—many people wanted them. There were riots in the stores as parents fought over the last dolls for their children. Some stores started wrapping the dolls in paper so that buyers would not fight over the ones they liked best. The Cabbage Patch craze went further to include clothing for the dolls and a younger generation of babies, including very small "preemie" babies.

Slang

gnarly great

rad extremely cool or attractive

bogus not good

airhead empty-headed

like no meaning; used as a filler

veg out do nothing

dweeb spineless, nerdy

chillin' relaxing

couch potato a person who watches a lot of TV

grodie disgusting

STRAP ON A SWATCH

■ Americans were telling time in style. Swiss company Asuag-SSIH hit it big with its line of durable watches, called Swatches. The company released Swatches to compete with cheap watches from Japan. Swatches were a hit. These ticking accessories became a must for Americans. The inexpensive plastic watches were available in many colors, patterns, and styles.

Fitness Crazy

In 1981, an Oscar-winning actor joined the fitness fad with the release of *Jane Fonda's Workout Book*. Fonda's book offered diet tips and exercise routines, and it gave general health information for women. Her book reached Americans who were aerobics crazy—mostly women who were eager to get into shape and be healthy. The book was a bestseller and was followed by cassette tapes of music to play while working out. There were also fitness studios and, later, a video to demonstrate the exercises. Americans handed over their money and cleared away the furniture in their family rooms so that they could "feel the burn" and shed the pounds.

Many other people cashed in on the fitness craze. Sneaker manufacturers introduced running shoes made with extra support for exercising.

Thousands of fitness clubs and gyms opened across the country to accommodate the growing number of men and women interested in bulking up or losing weight. Unlike many fads, the fitness craze continued for the rest of the century and into the next.

Rubik's Cube

Who would have imagined that a six-sided cube could cause so much fascination? Hungarian professor Erno Rubik had an idea that his Rubik's Cube would frustrate and delight puzzle lovers around the world. He invented the puzzle in 1975 as a way of teaching his students about three-dimensional objects. A few years later, he sold the puzzle worldwide. People first had to twist the rows of squares to scramble the colors. Then they had to figure out how to twist them back into position with only one color on each side. It seemed an impossible task at first. As the 1980s rolled on, people learned how to solve the puzzle. Then they concentrated on solving it faster. Some Rubik's Cube wizards could solve the puzzle in less than a minute. By July 1981, 10 million cubes had been sold in the U.S. alone.

■ Rubik's Cube became so popular that it was even made into a cartoon.

BREAK DANCING

■ The rise of rap music in the 1980s brought a new form of dancing to U.S. streets. Break dancing was introduced by inner-city African-American youth. Groups of people would gather at schoolyards or on street corners, turn up the hip-hop or rap music, and show off their moves. They often competed with each other, comparing their best tricks. Many did back flips and head spins. Others perfected jerky, robot-like maneuvers. Break dancing was so popular that movies were made about it. *Wild Style* (1982) paved the way for other break dancing movies, such as *Breakin'* (1984) and *Breakin' 2: Electric Boogaloo* (1984).

Chernobyl Disaster

In late April and May 1986, power plants in Norway, Finland, Sweden, and Denmark registered high levels of radiation. The scientists checked their plants but did not find any problems. As it turned out, the wind had carried radiation to their countries from the Ukraine. Scientists soon discovered that a catastrophe had occurred on April 26. A nuclear power plant near the city of Chernobyl had suffered an explosion in one of its reactors, releasing 100 million curies of radiation into the air. The power plant burned for two weeks, making it impossible to plug the leak.

Thirty-one people died from the initial explosion. Thousands more were killed from the gradual effects of radiation poisoning. About 40,000 cancer cases and around 6,500 deaths were blamed on the explosion. Farmland and cattle as far away as Western Europe and Scandinavia were contaminated. A true estimate of the damage from the explosion will not be known for a generation, when birth defects and illnesses from radiation will appear. Chernobyl was the worst nuclear accident in history.

■ The Chernobyl reactor was almost completely destroyed after the meltdown. To stop the spread of radiation, a shelter was built around the exposed radioactive material.

■ Anwar al-Sadat was one of the first leaders to strive for peace in the Middle East.

Anwar al-Sadat Assassinated

When Anwar al-Sadat became president of Egypt in 1970, he quickly built up his military strength. He engaged in the Arab-Israeli war in 1973. By 1977, Egypt was heavily in debt and underdeveloped. Peace was the answer. Sadat made a trip to Jerusalem and recognized Israel as an independent country. He was the first Arab leader to do so. In 1978, Sadat and the Israeli prime minister, Menachem Begin, shared the Nobel Peace Prize for their efforts to keep peace in the Middle East. They signed a peace treaty in 1979, which led to Israel's withdrawal from the Sinai Peninsula. Sadat's peacemaking with Israel made many other Arab leaders and religious **fundamentalists** angry. On October 6, 1981, Anwar al-Sadat was assassinated by religious fanatics in his own army.

Famine in Africa

In the African country of Ethiopia, many people could barely grow enough food to feed their families. Things got worse in 1984 and 1985. Eastern Africa, including Sudan and Ethiopia, suffered a terrible drought. All of the crops and many rivers and ponds dried up, leaving the people with nothing to eat or drink. Millions of people were in danger of starving. The government was focusing its attention and resources on the civil war it was fighting instead of helping its citizens. As images of the famine were broadcast on television, governments from around the world donated money and supplies to the devastated area. They could not provide enough for all the 6 million Ethiopians in need. Even with these efforts, an estimated 2 million people died of starvation by 1985, about half of whom lived in Ethiopia.

Tiananmen Square Massacre

At first, Chinese students marched for democracy. Then they demanded the removal of communist premier Li Peng and other officials. The government ordered the demonstrations to stop, but the students ignored it. On May 4, 1989, students and workers marched for democracy in Beijing. The government declared martial law, but the demonstrators would not back down. On June 3 and 4, the government took action. It ordered troops and tanks into Tiananmen Square to end the protesting once and for all. Some guess as many as 3,000 people were killed, although the government has never released any numbers. Around 10,000 people were injured in the fighting. Afterward, hundreds of people were arrested, tried, and executed.

This was not the first time communist China had resolved demonstrations this way. The level of violence in this case, as well as the presence of media, resulted in an international outcry. Countries around the world condemned the actions of the Chinese government.

A citizen confronts a convoy of tanks on the Avenue of Eternal Peace in Beijing.

Berlin Wall Falls

Millions of bright young people had escaped from communist East Germany to the West since 1949. The country did not intend to lose any more. In 1961, the 28-mile Berlin Wall was built to stop East Germans from leaving their country. After it was built, hundreds of people were killed trying to climb the wall to freedom. All that became

history on November 9, 1989. Just after 11:00 PM, the gate in the Berlin Wall was opened, and West and East Germans could pass freely through it. People danced, horns honked, and church bells rang. Some people knocked pieces of the wall off with hammers. Others cheered as they climbed over the wall. It was

the first time in decades that families split by the wall had seen each other. The relationship between East and West Germany warmed, and the two reunited as one country in 1990.

■ People gather in celebration as the Berlin Wall is dismantled.

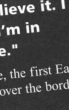

"I just can't believe it. I don't feel like I'm in prison anymore."

Angelika Wache, the first East German to cross over the border

DEADLY LEAK

■ On December 3, 1984, an invisible intruder attacked residents of Bhopal, India. Toxic gas leaked from a Union Carbide chemical plant. It burned people's eyes and suffocated them. Around 2,000 people died shortly after the accident, and another 2,000 eventually died from their injuries. In all, the gas made more than 200,000 people sick or permanently injured.

Union Carbide was criticized. Many people did not believe that the U.S. company had followed safety standards. Union Carbide settled all lawsuits against it with $470 million—about $150,000 for each person who died as a result of the leak. The Bhopal disaster became one of the worst industrial accidents in history.

Polish Solidarity

In the eighties, Polish workers began to fight for unions. This was the first time a Soviet bloc country had stood up for unions. Thousands of workers went on strike. The strike soon included 500,000 workers. They demanded independent labor unions and democratic elections. The government loosened restrictions on free speech and travel. It also made Solidarity legal. But the fight was not over.

In November, Polish General Wojciech Jaruzelski met with Solidarity leader Lech Walesa. They tried to negotiate terms,

but it was not enough for many workers. Solidarity had become 10 million people strong, and supporters were impatient for a union. Against Walesa's advice, the workers demanded that communism be wiped out of Poland. They had gone too far.

Within hours, on December 12, 1981, troops moved in. At least seven workers were killed, and thousands were arrested. Walesa spent more than a year in prison. After seventeen months of freedom for Polish citizens, Solidarity was over. This state of **martial law** stayed in place until 1983, the year Lech Walesa was given the Nobel Peace Prize.

Man of the Decade

In March 1985, Mikhail Gorbachev became leader of the Soviet Union. He promised to turn the country around, and he changed the Soviet Union completely. Gorbachev wanted to open his country up and rebuild it, with no more secrets. He called this openness *glasnost*. For the first time in decades, the media could question and challenge the government.

Certain parts of the USSR, such as the Ukraine, were allowed to become independent.

Gorbachev also announced that he would reduce military spending and focus on the well-being of Soviet citizens. He made it easier for citizens to buy a range of products, including clothing and food. This effort was called *perestroika*, or restructuring. The president's reforms led to the USSR becoming a democratic state.

It also led to its fall as a superpower. Years of strained relations with the West were put to rest. Gorbachev's new ideas led to him being named *Time* magazine's "Man of the Decade."

> "We will have to carry out profound transformations in the economy and in the entire system of social relations."
>
> Mikhail Gorbachev

Iran-Iraq War

Iran and Iraq are neighboring Muslim countries in the Middle East. Both export a lot of oil. While Iran was busy holding U.S. citizens as hostages in 1980, Iraq attacked. The attack went against a 1975 treaty and took over an important waterway between the two countries.

A war broke out between the two nations and lasted for eight years.

Oil resources and refining facilities were fought over during the war. Both Baghdad, the capital of Iraq, and Tehran, the capital of Iran, were bombed. Nearby countries became involved, lending their support to one side or the other. The U.S. also played a role in the war by

escorting supertankers through the Persian Gulf.

The Iran-Iraq War ended in a **stalemate,** when both sides finally agreed to a cease-fire on August 8, 1988. The war claimed the lives of a million people, many of them young soldiers.

■ A clergyman and his escort wear gas masks to protect themselves from the threat of chemical warfare.

ROYAL WEDDING

■ It was a fairy tale wedding, complete with a prince and princess. Around 750 million people watched Prince Charles marry Lady Diana Spencer on television July 29, 1981. Another million lined the streets, hoping to catch a glimpse of the royal couple. Britons were all too happy to forget, for a day, the country's economic troubles and unemployment. They cheered as 20-year-old Diana, dressed in a gown that cost a small fortune, kissed her new husband. Many saw Diana as refreshed hope for Britain. Her outgoing personality made her a role model for young people around the world.

Hostages Released

In 1979, Iranian terrorists took over the U.S. embassy in Tehran. Fifty-two Americans were taken hostage. These captives were seen as spies and enemies to the Iranians. They were much more to the Iranian leader, Ayatollah Khomeini. He used the hostages to get his way. At first, he wanted a fugitive brought back to Iran for punishment. Then he wanted the U.S. to release money that was frozen in U.S. banks. Instead of giving in, U.S. president

WELCOME BACK TO FREEDOM

■ After 444 days of captivity, the shaken hostages were happy to be free.

Jimmy Carter sent in troops.

President Carter sent commandos to Tehran to free the hostages. It was a disaster. A helicopter crash claimed the lives of eight soldiers. Other technical problems prevented the Americans from rescuing their **compatriots**. Americans lost faith in their leader, even though Carter continued to negotiate with Khomeini. The war between Iraq and Iran presented the only breakthrough. Iran needed money. The U.S. agreed to release 70 percent of Iran's funds in January 1981 if the hostages were let go. The hostages were freed, but Jimmy Carter's presidency was over. The U.S. hostages were released minutes after Ronald Reagan's **inauguration.**

Reagan's America

In 1980, Ronald Reagan went from being a star of the silver screen to a star of politics. In November, the Republican candidate beat out Jimmy Carter to become the president of the U.S. At sixty-nine years of age, Reagan was the oldest elected president.

Reagan's ideas were radical, and he quickly put them to work. He thought that economic success could best be achieved if businesses were left alone. He reduced taxes and relaxed regulations that had been in place for decades. To further strengthen the economy, Reagan cut spending. He wanted Americans and the rest of the world to see how strong the country was.

But the **Cold War** was still raging. Reagan wanted to make sure the U.S. could outgun the Soviet Union. He increased military spending in order to keep the country competitive. Americans supported Reagan's efforts, and the charismatic leader was re-elected in 1984. Despite a faltering economy, Reagan continued to fight communism through various programs. In the late eighties, he managed to ease some of the tension between the Soviet Union and the U.S. After

> "Government is not the solution to our problem; government is the problem."
>
> Ronald Reagan

lengthy discussions, Reagan and Soviet leader Mikhail Gorbachev agreed to get rid of some land-based nuclear missiles.

After fulfilling his maximum two terms in office, Reagan left the leadership to his vice president, George Bush. The Iran-Contra affair may have tarnished his image, but Ronald Reagan left politics as one of the most popular presidents ever.

President Shot

On March 30, 1981, as he was leaving a Washington hotel, President Ronald Reagan was shot in the chest. The gunman, John Hinckley, Jr., was obsessed with actor Jodie Foster and said the attack was a tribute to her.

■ Police and Secret Service agents dive on top of the president and James Brady.

He was ruled insane and was not convicted for the crime. The president was lucky and recovered quickly. Public support for the leader was enormous. He joked with the press about it, saying to his wife, Nancy, "Honey, I forgot to duck." Others injured in the shooting included a Secret Service agent, a police officer, and press secretary James Brady. Brady suffered permanent brain damage as a result of the assault.

GERALDINE FERRARO A FIRST

■ Geraldine Ferraro was a New York lawyer before being elected to Congress in 1978. She was re-elected until 1984. Then Ferraro became the first woman chosen as a nominee for vice president in a major political party. Walter Mondale, the Democratic nominee for the presidency, chose Ferraro himself. Many people thought running with a female vice president would draw the female voters away from President Reagan. However, the Mondale-Ferraro team lost the November election. Ferraro returned to her private life. She bid unsuccessfully to become a senator from New York in 1992 and 1998.

Iran Contra

In 1986, reports leaked out that U.S. parts for jets and tanks, along with ammunition and missiles, had been secretly sold to Iran. U.S. officials hoped that Iran would help free some U.S. hostages who were held by Lebanese terrorists. The deal went against a law passed by Congress that **forbade** selling arms to Iran, which was an enemy to the U.S. Some of the money made from the sale went to helping rebel guerrillas

fighting against the communist government in Nicaragua. This was against another policy forbidding military assistance to the rebels, called contras.

When the illegal action was discovered, Americans were shocked. They were amazed that the U.S. military was dealing with the Iranian leader. People were also shocked that such an illegal activity, which was dubbed the Iran-Contra affair, could be connected to the White House. Highly

respected military personnel, including Oliver North and Rear Admiral John M. Poindexter, were investigated. President Reagan denied knowing of the affair, but critics were not sure he was being truthful. The Iran-Contra affair made many people question the government's honesty, and it damaged President Reagan's reputation with U.S. citizens.

Star Wars

The Cold War was in full swing in the early 1980s. The U.S. and the Soviet Union were building up their supplies of nuclear weapons. The fear of nuclear war motivated leaders to develop new weapons to protect their countries. In March 1983,

President Reagan announced his plan to defend the U.S. against a nuclear attack from the USSR. He called it the Strategic Defense Initiative. It would use the highest technological equipment to shoot down nuclear missiles before they reached the U.S. This plan involved equipment

on Earth as well as satellites in space. The plan soon became known as "Star Wars." The defense plan cost the government a great deal of money to research and prepare. Some people thought "Star Wars" would make the nuclear arms race worse. Others supported the idea, saying it was the only way to protect against nuclear weapons. In the late eighties, politics between the USSR and the U.S. changed. The Cold War thawed, and such a defense system became unnecessary.

■ Many people protested the Star Wars program, fearing it would escalate the arms race.

ABSCAM SCANDAL

■ The Federal Bureau of Investigation (FBI) suspected that some members of Congress were abusing their authority. To investigate their claims, a handful of FBI agents pretended to be rich Arabs and contacted the politicians. The undercover agents asked for political favors in return for money. The operation was called ABSCAM, a combination of "Abdul," who was one of the phony Arabs in the sting, and "scam." In February 1980, the results of the operation became public. The agents had secretly filmed their meetings with the members of Congress. The media gained access to the tapes, and the public watched as their officials filled their own pockets with dirty money. Several of the corrupt lawmakers were charged for their crimes.

WORLD FOCUS

ASSASSINATIONS

In the 1980s, many world leaders were the targets of assassins. Sometimes the attackers were linked to international terrorism. In other instances, they acted on their own. On March 24, 1980, Archbishop Oscar Romero, an outspoken human-rights activist, was killed while conducting mass at a hospital chapel in Central America.

Two months later, Pope John Paul II was shot twice in the stomach while riding in an open car through the streets of Rome, Italy. He recovered. His would-be assassin was an escaped criminal from Turkey who was later sentenced to life in prison.

Other prominent people assassinated during the 1980s include Malcolm H. Kerr, the president of the American University of Beirut, Lebanon; Indira Gandhi, the prime minister of India; and Olaf Palme, the prime minister of Sweden.

Secrets for Sale

In the 1980s, U.S. secrets were for sale. One of the most serious cases of **espionage** was that of John Walker, Jr. He was a naval officer in 1968, and he used his position and expertise in nuclear submarines to start selling classified information to the Soviets. He drew on the help and support of his brother, who was an engineer for a defense contractor; his son, who was a U.S. Navy lieutenant; and his best friend, who was an ex-navy officer. Walker's ex-wife turned him in and exposed one of the longest-running spy rings in history. All four participants received life sentences in 1985.

Another spy case involved Jonathan Jay Pollard. This case was not motivated by money. It was "moral espionage." Pollard was a naval-intelligence analyst who began spying for Israel in 1984. While the U.S. shared information with its ally, it withheld some sensitive information. Pollard was a **Zionist**, and he felt that it was his moral duty to fill in the details for the Israelis. In 1987, Pollard received a life sentence for espionage. His wife received five years in prison as an accomplice.

George Bush Becomes President

■ President Bush stands proud during his inauguration.

In 1980, George Bush began serving as President Reagan's vice president. In 1988, after Ronald Reagan retired, Bush was elected president. His support of Reagan told foreign allies that policies would not change much with the new leader. Like Reagan, Bush took action when necessary. In 1989, he ordered troops to invade Panama in Central America and arrest its leader, General Manuel Noriega. He also joined the Persian Gulf War to fight Saddam Hussein of Iraq.

At home, President Bush promised Americans that he would not raise taxes. It was a promise he could not keep. Huge budget deficits made it necessary to increase taxes.

The economy was sluggish, and unemployment was high. President Bush was criticized and blamed by the opposition and voters alike. They put their feelings into votes at the ballot boxes. Bush lost the 1992 presidential election to Democrat Bill Clinton.

Cyberpunk Writer

In 1984, William Gibson introduced the world to cyberspace. His books were in the genre of cyberpunk. In these novels, space is colonized and people live forever. Other cyberpunk books, such as *Blade Runner*, were made into movies.

Gibson's novel *Neuromancer* presents a world of technology and huge corporations that control society and threaten people's rights. The heroes of the novel have mechanically and electronically enhanced bodies. They work in cyberspace, which is the world created by the meeting of computer networks and the human mind. *Neuromancer* is thought to be one of the most important science fiction books of the 1980s. In it, Gibson introduces phrases such as "virtual reality" and "cyberspace."

The novel won Gibson the Nebula and Hugo Awards, two of the most prestigious science fiction awards. Gibson later released a collection of short stories called *Burning Chrome*. This collection contained "Johnny Mnemonic," which was made into a movie in 1994.

Literary Excellence

Poet and author Alice Walker wrote her first collection of published poems in only one week. Her writing often had the same theme—oppressed African-American women trying to make a better life for themselves in the 1900s. In 1982, the world took notice of her talents. She published *The Color Purple*, which is written as a series of letters that an abused woman named Celie writes to God and to her sister. The strong characters and touching story attracted readers from coast to coast. The book earned Walker an American Book Award and a Pulitzer Prize. It was made into a successful movie starring Whoopi Goldberg and Danny Glover in 1985. The film won a Directors Guild of America Award for Outstanding Directorial Achievement and a Golden Globe Award for best

Since the 1960s Alice Walker has been active in the civil rights movement.

actress for Goldberg. It also brought recognition to the talented author. Walker later wrote *The Temple of My Familiar* (1989) and *Possessing the Secret of Joy* (1992).

THE JOY LUCK CLUB

The Joy Luck Club was a place where Chinese women could meet and talk. Amy Tan's 1989 novel of the same name follows the lives of four Chinese immigrant women and their Americanized daughters. The mothers worry about their daughters' withdrawal from their Chinese culture, but the daughters do not understand their mothers concerns. The mothers talk about their battles to overcome traditional women's roles in China, and the daughters try to find equality in their relationships and professions. The tensions between the generations create a fascinating piece of fiction that is based on fact. *The Joy Luck Club* was Tan's first novel, and it brought her a great deal of attention and acclaim, including a Los Angeles Times Book Award and a National Book Award.

Salman Rushdie was a talented writer living in Britain. In 1988, he received more attention than he wanted when his book The Satanic Verses *was published.*

Rushdie's book follows two Muslims who survive an airplane bombing. One of the men grows horns, hooves, and a tail. The other grows a halo and dreams of meeting prophets, including Mahound, which is a **derogatory** *name for Islamic prophet Muhammad. Rushdie's book brought an instant reaction from Muslims, who felt the author was attacking their faith. Demonstrations, riots, and book burnings followed. The book was banned in several Islamic countries. In 1989, Iran's leader, Ayatollah Khomeini, declared that Rushdie and anyone who helped publish the book should be brought to death. The* **bounty** *on Rushdie's head reached more than $2 million.*

Rushdie apologized and said that he followed the Islamic faith, but the Ayatollah would not lift the bounty. The author went into hiding for two years. Then he began to make unscheduled appearances and gave a few interviews. By 1995, Rushdie was making more and more public appearances. After a decade, he was still cautious. No one claimed the bounty, which was officially withdrawn in 1998.

The King of Terror

By the 1980s, Stephen King had succeeded in scaring U.S. readers with every page they turned. He used ordinary events, such as peer pressure or a children's game, and turned them into terrifying stories. King's book *Christine*, published in 1983, centers on a strange car. *It* (1986) follows a murderous clown in a small town. *Misery* (1987) tells the story of a writer and an obsessed fan who forces him to write. King's books have a large following, and fans eagerly await his next novel. Many of King's books have been made into television or big-screen movies. But there is more to Stephen King than just horror. In 1976, he tried his hand at science fiction and released *The Gunslinger,* which was followed by *The Drawing of the Three* (1989). King has written several other books under the pen name Richard Bachman, including *Skeleton Crew* (1985).

■ Stephen King is one of America's most popular authors. His books have been translated into more than thirty languages.

The Books of Judy Blume

Judy Blume wrote realistic books for young adults and children. Her skill came from being able to remember what it was like to be a child growing up. Her first well-known novel in the 1970s was *Are You There, God? It's Me, Margaret,* a series of "conversations" a young girl has with God. This story hit home with young readers. Blume received letters from readers who said they also talked to God, "just like Margaret."

Some people did not think Blume's books were appropriate for children. She wrote honestly and frankly about issues that affected and concerned children. Divorce, losing loved ones, and the changes that take place as children become young adults are all represented in her books. Judy Blume wrote several popular children's books during the 1970s and 1980s. Her best-known works include *Superfudge* (1980), *Tiger Eyes* (1981), *As Long as We're Together* (1987), and the sequel to *Superfudge*, *Fudge-a-Mania* (1990).

Virtual Invention

In 1984, "virtual reality" became a reality. A twenty-four-year-old inventor named Jaron Lanier and his company VPL Research created the first virtual reality environment. He created the headset, gloves, and suits, along with the software for "cybernauts" to explore while playing the game. Participants could see, hear, and interact with a digital world. Early VR programs had their bugs, including a cartoonish world and some headaches and nausea from the headset. Yet people were still drawn to the possibilities that virtual reality presented. By the 1990s, many other companies were working on virtual reality. The military and airlines used the simulator concept to train pilots. VR games and other recreational three-dimensional movies were offered as well. Virtual reality took the computer experience to the next level.

■ Virtual reality systems have been used to train architects, help the disabled, and even create art.

> "For over a decade we've been looking at our computerized world through a fish bowl called a monitor. Virtual reality invites us to step inside a 3-D view of this world and feel our way around."
>
> A journalist writing about virtual reality

COMPUTER CRAZY

■ Before the 1980s, most Americans could not afford a computer. In 1981, IBM introduced its personal computer (PC). These desktop computers were run by an Intel microprocessor that held the information to make the computer work. The computers used MS-DOS, which is Microsoft's operating system of programs used to run the machines. These components were soon reproduced and sold to other companies. IBM clones that ran just like authentic IBMs were quickly created and sold. IBM had not taken steps to prevent Intel and Microsoft from selling their products to companies that were looking to copy IBM's success. By 1984, about 3 million PCs were being sold each year. By the mid-1990s, about 90 percent of the world's computers were IBMs or copies.

■ Sally Ride was instrumental in designing and testing the remote arm for NASA's shuttles.

A Ride in Space

Sally Ride was a professional tennis player before she became star-struck. She left sports to finish her Ph.D. in astrophysics. On June 18, 1983, Ride became the first U.S. woman in space. During the six-day flight, Ride launched communications satellites and tested the shuttle's remote arm. She went into orbit again on October 5, 1984. A few years later, she was asked to join the commission investigating the *Challenger* explosion of 1986. Ride resigned from the space program in 1987. She became director of the California Space Institute at the Scripps Institution of Oceanography, as well as a physics professor at the University of California in San Diego. She was inducted into the National Women's Hall of Fame in 1988.

Snapshots from Space

NASA launched two space probes to explore the solar system in 1977. In November 1980, the unmanned *Voyager 1* probe sent incredible pictures back to Earth. In its journey through the solar system, the probe passed by Saturn. The photographs showed that the planet's rings were actually made of many smaller rings. It also discovered eight moons that were too tiny to be seen from Earth. *Voyager 1* showed what scientists on Earth had seen only as spots of light. In 1989, *Voyager 2* passed Neptune, sending back rare images of the planet. The space probes offered important information that astronomers would not have received otherwise.

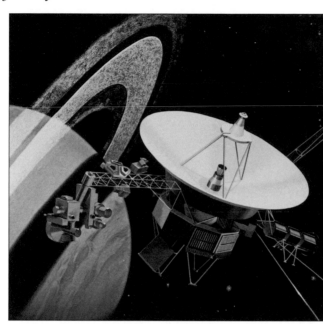

■ The *Voyager* probes used cameras, radio transmitters, and sunlight to study Saturn's rings.

■ Dr. Robert Jarvik invented the polyurethane heart. The first time it was used, it kept a calf alive for 268 days.

Handing Out Hearts

On December 2, 1982, Utah doctors gave Barney Clark an early Christmas gift—a new Jarvik-7 heart. A team of eighteen surgeons implanted the first artificial heart in a human at the University of Utah Medical Center in Salt Lake City. Before then, an artificial heart had been placed only in sheep and cattle. The operation took seven-and-a-half hours, and the plastic heart held up well. But complications set in soon after the operation. Clark suffered from seizures in the first week and had problems with his lungs and liver. This was likely because of less blood flow in these areas during surgery. The patient lived for 112 days after the operation. Over the next ten years, the artificial heart was improved upon and used for patients waiting for heart transplants.

WORLD FOCUS

AIDS IDENTIFIED

In the early 1980s, mysterious illnesses were being reported around the world. Doctors could not explain why so many people were dying from treatable illnesses such as pneumonia and skin cancer. By 1982, doctors had examined sufferers and realized that the problem lay with their immune systems. The immune system helps the body fight infections and disease. The new condition, called acquired immunodeficiency syndrome, or AIDS, prevented the immune system from doing its job.

It was thought to be caused by HIV, or human immunodeficiency virus, in the body. There was a chance that people with HIV would develop AIDS.

By December 1982, 1,600 cases of AIDS had been reported worldwide. The number of cases was doubling every six months. HIV is passed through body fluids. Any activity that involves sharing body fluids is considered risky. People became terrified that they would develop AIDS. Many people, including Americans, started to alter their behavior to keep themselves safe.

Carl Lewis Races for Gold

Alabama native Carl Lewis won nine Olympic gold medals between 1984 and 1996. He won four straight gold medals in the long jump. Lewis was the second Olympian in history to win the same event in four consecutive Olympic Games.

Lewis had his best showing ever at the 1984 Olympic Games in Los Angeles. He won a gold medal in the 100- and 200-meter dashes. He also helped the 4 x100-meter relay team win the gold. Then he took home the gold medal in the long jump. This sort of triumph had not been seen since American Jesse Owens won four medals in the 1936 Games. Lewis became a hero, but he was not finished yet. At the 1987 World Championships, he won the long jump and was on the winning 4 x100-meter relay team. The next year, Lewis again won the long jump as well as the

■ Carl Lewis is one of the greatest sprinters and long jumpers in track and field history.

100-meter race after Canadian Ben Johnson tested positive for banned substances. Lewis finished second in the 200-meter race. Throughout his career, Carl Lewis won medals and made history. He retired from competition in 1997.

Athletes Stay Home from Olympics

The 1980 Olympic Games in Moscow, USSR, were not a success. The USSR had invaded Afghanistan, and many countries were angry. U.S. President Jimmy Carter wanted to show the world what he felt about the invasion. He asked the Olympic committee to move the Games out of Moscow. The committee refused. Carter decided to **boycott** the games. Fifty-nine other countries followed his lead.The boycott disappointed many athletes. They had trained hard for the competition but now could not compete at the Games. They had to wait another four years for the next Olympics. It also meant that the Olympic medalists that year were not necessarily the best in the world. To get back at the Americans, the Soviet teams boycotted the 1984 Olympics held in Los Angeles, California.

FLO-JO TAKES OLYMPICS BY STORM

▬ Since she was 7 years old, Florence Griffith Joyner had trained in track and field. She won a silver medal in the 200-meter race at the 1984 Olympics, and then went into semi-retirement. She returned to track in 1987 to place second at the World Championship Games. The following year, Flo-Jo set world records at the Olympic Games. She was the first female athlete to win four medals at an Olympics. She won the gold in the 100-, 200-, and 4x100-meter relay races. She also won a silver in the 4x400-meter race. Her amazing performance, along with her glamorous and eye-catching style, made her a star. She became one of the highest paid sports figures in the world. She retired from track in 1989.

Flo-Jo died suddenly on September 21, 1998, at the age of 38. Her passing shocked her fans and family.

American Conquers Tour de France

In 1984, Greg LeMond finished third at the **grueling** Tour de France cycling race. The Tour de France is a 2,400-mile race that takes between twenty-five and thirty days to complete. Fewer than half the cyclists who enter finish the course. LeMond was not satisfied with his result, although it was the best finish for a non-European cyclist up to that point. In 1986, he became the first American to win the race. A hunting accident in 1987 threatened his racing career, but he worked through the injury and competed again in 1989. He won by eight seconds—the smallest victory margin in the history of the race. LeMond went on to win the Tour de France again in 1990. A rare progressive muscle disorder forced the amazing cyclist to retire in 1994.

Boys of Summer on Strike

On June 11, 1981, the baseball season came to a sudden end. Problems between owners and players resulted in a players' strike. The owners had tried to restrict free agency. Free agency allows players to have agents help them with their contracts. If they want to move, their agent helps negotiate a new contract with a new team. The owners said that free agency was costing them too much money. But the players refused to take the field without their right to become free agents. It took until July 31 to settle the strike. It was one of the longest strikes in baseball's history.

▬ Disheartened baseball fans mourn the loss of one of their favorite pastimes.

Islanders on Top

The New York Islanders dominated professional hockey in the early eighties. Rather than trading their superstars, as many other teams had done, the Islanders recruited in small towns and from junior hockey teams. They found three important rookies in Mike Bossy, Denis Potvin, and Bryan Trottier. These men and other young, fast players led them to the Stanley Cup championships.

Each line of the Islanders was strong and able to score goals. They could also defend their net, even while short-handed. In the 1983 series, the Islanders stood their ground against twenty power plays by the Edmonton Oilers. The Oilers did not score once during those power plays. On the other hand, when the Islanders had a man advantage, they put the puck in the net. In the 1981 series, the team scored a record thirty-one goals during power plays. This drive and talent helped the Islanders win the Stanley Cup for four straight seasons, starting in 1980.

■ Islander Bob Nystrom scores a winning goal.

Kareem of the Crop

Ferdinand Lewis Alcindor, Jr. led the University of California basketball team to three straight championships. This piqued the attention of the National Basketball League (NBA), and Alcindor was offered a contract with the Milwaukee Bucks.

In 1968, Alcindor became a member of the Muslim faith, and in 1971, he changed his name to Kareem Abdul-Jabbar. He played for the Bucks from 1969 to 1975. Then he was traded to the Los Angeles Lakers. There, the 7-feet-2-inch center led the team to five championships. Abdul-Jabbar was known for his signature "sky hook" shot. It was hard for his opponents to block, and he rarely missed. When he retired in 1989, Abdul-Jabbar was the all-time points leader in the NBA with 38,387 in 1,560 professional games. He had led his team to the NBA finals and was named the Most Valuable Player (MVP) six times. He was one of the best players to ever take to the court and was elected to the Basketball Hall of Fame in 1995.

The Fall of a Hero

Pete Rose was one of the greatest baseball players ever. He played both infield and outfield, and his aggressive base running earned him the nickname "Charlie Hustle." He was the rookie of the year in 1963, and he held several records in his twenty-four years of play. He beat Ty Cobb's record for career hits, with 4,191. In 1973, Rose was named the National League MVP, and he played on seventeen All-Star teams at five different positions. Rose retired from playing for the Cincinnati Reds in 1986 and from managing the Reds in 1989.

In 1989, Rose was suspended from baseball for life. He was suspected of betting on sports, including baseball. Rose insisted that he had never bet on baseball, but he agreed not to challenge the ban. In 1991, the baseball commissioner announced that anyone banned from baseball could not be **inducted** into the baseball Hall of Fame. The man who had helped make baseball what it is would never be recognized. Baseball fans and Rose himself continue to petition to change the ruling.

FIGHTING TO THE TOP

▇ Michael Gerard Tyson learned to box in 1980. He had been sent to reform school after being charged with burglaries and robberies. Following an impressive amateur boxing career, Tyson turned professional in 1985. That year, he won fourteen bouts, eleven of which were first-round knockouts. On November 22, 1986, the heavyweight belt changed hands, when Tyson challenged the Canadian world champion, Trevor Berbick. In the second round, the powerful Tyson defeated Berbick with a sledgehammer punch. At 20 years old, Mike Tyson became the youngest world heavyweight champion ever. By 1989, his incredible win-loss record was 37-0, with 33 knockouts. Tyson was unstoppable, or at least almost so. His legal problems, including assault and rape convictions, jeopardized his career into the 1990s. After spending time in jail, Tyson returned to the ring in 1996 to win both the World Boxing Association and World Boxing Council titles. Tyson is known as one of the hardest punchers in the history of professional boxing.

Top Tennis Player

In 1982, the Women's Tennis Association ranked Martina Navratilova the world's best female player. She kept that title for four straight years. In this time, Navratilova won twelve Grand Slam tennis tournaments and boasted an incredible win-loss record of 427-14. Her strength was something not often seen in women's tennis. Her serve was clocked at 90 miles an hour. In 1975, the eighteen-year-old defected to the U.S. from Czechoslovakia. In 1986, she returned to Prague, where she led the U.S. tennis team to victory over Czechoslovakia at the Federation Cup. By 1992, Navratilova had won more than 158 championships, more than any other tennis player in history.

▇ Martina Navratilova celebrates another victory at Wimbledon.

Vietnam Memorial

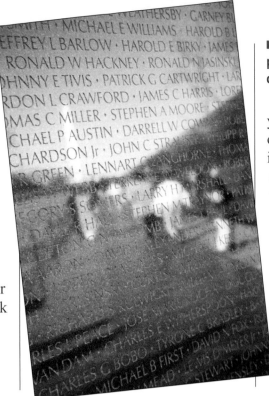

Maya Yang Lin won a contest that affected thousands of people. The architecture student was challenged to design a memorial to the killed and missing soldiers of the Vietnam War. Lin's design was not a typical tribute to fallen war heroes. It was simple—two black granite walls in the ground with the names of more than 50,000 U.S. soldiers engraved on them. The memorial was debated for

■ The Vietman Memorial pays tribute to the soldiers who died in the name of democracy.

years. Many people were opposed to America's involvement in Vietnam and did not want to honor those who had fought there. Others were strongly in favor of the memorial because it would recognize the sacrifice that thousands of Americans had made. The Washington memorial was dedicated in November 1982. It became a place for veterans to say goodbye to their lost friends.

HAVING IT ALL

■ If the eighties were known for anything, it was excess. The U.S. culture was full of money, glamour, and fancy belongings. But the quest for money was not seen as greedy. It was admired and encouraged. Beginning in 1982, there were more than 100,000 new millionaires each year. There were also fifty-one U.S. billionaires with money to burn. Instead of making money by producing or selling a product, eighties successes often managed the shift in ownership of companies or refinanced corporations. These newly rich Americans spent money freely, buying enormous houses, expensive cars, and the best of everything. But all good things come to an end. The economy changed, people lost their jobs, and the market crashed. Once Americans recovered from the bust after the boom, they stepped more cautiously into the 1990s.

Environmentally Friendly

In the 1980s, Americans became more environmentally aware. Several discoveries caught the country's attention, including the depleting ozone layer, overflowing landfill sites, disappearing rain forests, and acid rain. People's actions were causing these problems. People had to change their habits before it was too late. Americans were encouraged to recycle their plastic, paper, and glass products. Newspapers also were recycled. Rhode Island went so far as to make recycling mandatory in homes.

Environmental societies were formed to prevent any more damage. The groups of the 1980s set the environmental movement in motion, and they continued to fight for the environment into the next century.

■ Every day, millions of tons of garbage are buried in landfills around the world. Sights like this inspire people to protect the environment.

Equal Rights Amendment Defeated

The Equal Rights Amendment (ERA) was proposed to guarantee women equal rights under the law. This change to the Constitution had been proposed since 1923, and it had already been approved by Congress in 1972. In the mid-1970s, people began to protest the amendment. Some people, including many women, argued that the change would threaten the stability of

■ **Since 1982, the ERA has been reintroduced in Congress many times. It has never been passed.**

U.S. families. Women, they said, would be encouraged to walk away from their roles as wives and mothers.

For the amendment to be included in the Constitution, thirty-eight state legislatures had to approve it. It received support from only thirty-five states. Congress extended the deadline, but opposition continued. On June 30, 1982, the ERA was **quashed.** However, the spirit of the amendment carried on, as women's rights were guaranteed in several states.

Homelessness

The problem of homelessness exploded in the 1980s. It often affected entire families. The government had cut back aid programs, and many U.S. families did not have access to support. The economy changed from being industry-based to being service-based. Thousands of people lost their high-paying factory jobs. Service jobs, such as waiting on tables and cleaning, could not support families. By mid-decade, around 14 percent of the population lived below the **poverty line**. In 1985, Americans got together to help ease the burden on homeless people. On May 25, 6 million people joined hands, creating a chain stretching from coast to coast. "Hands Across America" raised $20 million for emergency aid, revised existing social programs, and introduced new programs.

"We were wards of the state. Imagine belonging to the state?... Can you come home to the state? Can it hold you and make you feel safe?"

A homeless woman

Woman Benched

On September 21, 1981, Sandra Day O'Connor made history. She became the first woman to serve on the bench of the Supreme Court. President Reagan's appointment of a woman to the highest court in the country surprised many people.

While nearly half of American women worked outside the home at this time, very few held positions of power. O'Connor was up to the challenge. She had previously been an **appellate** court judge in Arizona. With this appointment, O'Connor became one of the most influential women in the country.

Black Monday

On October 19, 1987, U.S. stock markets witnessed a plunge of 22 percent. This was almost double the fall of 1929, which set the Great Depression in motion. In one day, 604.5 million shares in companies were traded—more than double the previous record. The enormous drop cost stockholders around $500 billion. Many people lost everything they owned.

> "What crashed was more than just the market. It was the Reagan illusion: the idea that there could be a defense buildup and tax cuts without a price, that the country could live beyond its means indefinitely."
>
> Time, November 2, 1987

Stock prices began to fall around the world. People waited nervously to see if this stock market crash, called Black Monday, would cause another economic depression.

The Federal Reserve Board took action. It put cash into the market, and banks started lending money again. Several companies began buying back their own stocks. These events, which happened within a few days of the crash, helped the market recover. Confidence built again, and the market stabilized. Still, it took about two years for the stock market to reach the level it was at before Black Monday.

American Reversal

Until the 1980s, the U.S. had a strong economy. The country had exported goods, ranging from clothes to metals, to the rest of the world. Due to an economic downswing, the U.S. had to buy many of these products from other countries in the eighties. To battle the recession, companies laid off employees and looked to the government for assistance. Americans experienced the first standard-of-living decline since World War II. The country's already high unemployment rate went higher. President Reagan promised to "put America back to work." He cut taxes and spending to help bring money into the U.S. The unemployment numbers dropped, and inflation remained steady. The economy began to grow after the slump in the early eighties. But the government tactics backfired. With the tax and spending cuts, there was not enough money coming in. The trade deficit grew from $19.7 billion to $119.8 billion between 1980 and 1989.

■ United Auto Workers Union President Douglas Fraser contemplates the negative effects of the trade deficit.

AT&T Breaks Up

In 1982, communications giant AT&T agreed to break up into smaller companies.

The government was concerned that the company had almost complete control of the telecommunications market. The Justice Department launched an **antitrust** lawsuit against AT&T because it had violated the rules against one company forming a monopoly. After a seven-year court battle, AT&T agreed to give up control of twenty-two regional telephone companies. It was able to keep Western Electric, its manufacturing business, and Bell Laboratories, its long-distance business. These components made the company the most money. After the settlement was reached, AT&T was able to enter the lucrative computer and electronics markets.

■ Despite the breakup of AT&T, telephones continued to ring.

Shell-out for Chrysler

In January 1980, President Carter signed the Chrysler Loan Guarantee bill. This was a $1.5 billion bailout for the struggling automotive manufacturer. Chrysler was America's seventeenth-largest company and had lost $207 million in the last quarter of 1979. U.S. cars were not selling as well as reliable, gas-efficient Japanese cars. President Reagan later tried to restrict Japanese imports, but Japanese manufacturers built factories in the U.S. and continued to make cars.

To deal with this problem, Lee Iacocca, the tough chairman of Chrysler, set out to put the company on track. Many workers were laid off so the company could survive. In 1984, thanks to a turnaround plan, Chrysler posted a first-quarter profit of $705 million. The company had recovered from its tough time and paid off the government loan—seven years ahead of schedule. The government had made a profit of $350 million in interest.

FARMING FALLS

■ Tough times hit U.S. farmers in the 1980s. In 1987, prices for agricultural goods dropped, and interest rates soared. Approximately 24,000 farmers were forced off their land. Banks foreclosed on farms that had been in families for generations. Independent farms were **consolidated** into huge agribusinesses. Also, since 1977, the percentage of farmers had dropped 9 percent. This brought the number of people growing crops to the lowest level since the Civil War. Those farmers who kept their land struggled to make ends meet.

■ Jeans were originally worn by people who lived and worked in the countryside. Many Americans wore jeans, but few designers had bothered to add denim to their lines. In the 1980s, clothing designers discovered denim. Successful designers, including Calvin Klein and Gloria Vanderbilt, released their identifiable brand-name jeans—the designer's label was visible on the waistband or pocket of the pants. These new jeans were

Superstar Style

M any U.S. style trends have been set by fashion-forward entertainers. In the 1980s, teenage girls were glued to their television sets, memorizing outfits and hairstyles worn by such stars as Madonna. Hair tied with pieces of mesh allowed dark roots to show through dyed blonde locks. Ripped clothes looked like they came from a thrift store, but the designer labels on them made

■ Madonna lets her eighties style shine through in the movie *Desperately Seeking Susan*.

them hot sellers. Eighties fashion was about pushing limits. Teens across the nation showed off their midriffs with half-shirts. They sported lots of make-up, crimped their hair, and even wore underwear as outerwear! To top off the latest look, chunky jewelry, including crucifixes, hung from long necklaces made of beads or fake pearls.

■ The arrival of designer jeans marked a casual shift in the world of fashion.

much more expensive than jeans had ever been before, but Americans were willing to pay for the name. Some jeans were pre-torn to give them the fashionably tattered look.

The eighties jean fads included stonewashed jeans. These jeans were dark blue with light streaks all over them. They embraced the worn or "washed-out" look that fashion-conscious Americans loved. Some manufacturers even added numerous zippers that had no purpose. Michael Jackson's zippered jackets helped this fad become especially popular.

Preppie Power

Y uppies dominated the 1980s. Yuppies, which stands for "young urban professionals," had a great deal of money and were not afraid to spend it on looking good. These successful Americans were doctors, computer technicians, engineers, and entrepreneurs, and their clothing and accessories displayed their income.

Women wore pearls as everyday accessories, along with cardigans and long, stylish skirts. Men kept up their flawless appearance with perfectly pressed dress pants and expensive shirts. As the eighties neared an end, so did the popularity of the preppie look. A new craze called grunge took its place and lasted into the nineties.

FITNESS FASHION

The fitness craze of the eighties and the popularity of disco dance filtered into fashion. Movie stars from *Dirty Dancing*, *Fame*, and *Flashdance* made the look of workout clothing fashionable. Before this decade, only serious dancers wore legwarmers to keep their muscles from tightening up. Now all sorts of people wore them. Legwarmers came in every imaginable color and pattern, and Americans matched them with their outfits. Fashion-aware Americans wore legwarmers over their pants.

The 1983 movie *Flashdance* made wearing ripped clothing acceptable. Americans wore big sweatshirts over workout tops. Actor Jennifer Beals brought the casual look to accepting Americans.

Mimicking Miami

The success of Don Johnson's hit television show *Miami Vice* turned the spotlight on his sense of fashion. His simple and comfortable way of dressing gave men an easy and fun fashion to follow. Trendy men wore light pants with matching jackets, which were worn over pastel T-shirts, rather than button-down dress shirts. Mesh shoes did not require socks. Shaving also was unnecessary. A day's worth of stubble finished off this casual, rugged look.

Heads Up Fashion

After Tom Cruise wore them in *Risky Business* and Corey Hart sang about them in "Sunglasses at Night," Americans needed the perfect pair of shades. Ray-Ban sunglasses became very popular with both men and women. People wore them indoors and outside. Another important accessory was the headband. In the fitness-crazy decade, headbands or sweatbands became the style. Stars such as John Travolta in *Staying Alive* and Olivia Newton-John in her "Physical" video made the headband a must.

Headbands helped draw attention to the "radical" hairstyles of the eighties. Crimping irons were a necessity for women. This wavy iron produced a kinked effect on hair. Another fad was messy and spiky hairstyles. But they were not easy to achieve. Men and women used a new product called mousse to hold the style they wanted.

■ Don Johnson's laid-back attitude became as popular as his fashion style.

Castro Sends Cubans to America

In 1980, Cuban President Fidel Castro loosened policies that made immigration to the U.S. illegal. He opened up the country's northern ports and invited Cubans who had already left the country to pick up their relatives at Mariel. Cuban Americans flocked to the port by boat. But they were not reunited with family. Castro would not allow them to leave without taking "undesirables" back to the U.S. with them. A great number of these "undesirables" were criminals

> "Few boats are getting any relatives out. I didn't see anybody hugging and kissing at Mariel."
>
> A U.S. skipper

■ Fidel Castro was admired by many of his fellow Cubans for his open opposition to U.S. foreign policies.

or mentally ill. Cuba continued this policy for months.

Relations between the U.S. and Cuba had not been strong before this. Now, the U.S. government was angry. This action went against its immigration policy and suggested the U.S. did not have control over its borders. The boatlift was declared illegal. As the boats returned to Florida, the Cubans were held in camps. Their arrival caused serious relocation problems. Around 125,000 Cubans had moved to Florida. In September 1980, Castro closed the ports again without offering any explanation.

War on Smuggling

The smuggling market was strong in the 1980s. For some smugglers, the product was unusual. For a fee, smugglers offered to sneak people into the U.S. to avoid having them go through the lengthy immigration process. On June 23, 1982, thirty-eight smugglers were charged with sneaking illegal **aliens** into the country. Undercover agents posing as drivers transported the aliens. This way they had been able to watch the

operations and find out who was involved. The people arrested had a great business—through them, more than 24,000 illegal aliens entered the U.S. each year. Most of the aliens were from Mexico and were headed for Illinois, California, Michigan, and New York. The smugglers' profits for providing this service reached around $24 million per year.

■ Despite efforts to curb illegal immigration, unlawful entry remains a problem.

Immigration Reform Act of 1986

In the 1980s, immigration received more national attention than it had since the 1920s. For five years, politicians and everyday Americans debated the pending immigration changes. Many people feared that loose immigration policies would result in fewer jobs for

■ Even under the restrictive Immigration Reform Act, many people still immigrate to the U.S.

U.S. citizens. By 1986, the Immigration Reform Act passed into legislation. The basic structure of the previous immigration policy was not changed, and legal immigration continued to grow. The policy aimed at reducing the number of illegal aliens in the country. It held four provisions— **amnesty**, requirements that employers check that new employees are eligible to work in the U.S., tough penalties for people who hire illegal aliens, and a provision that made it easier for fruit growers to import foreign agricultural workers.

Within two-and-a-half years of an immigrant's acceptance, he or she had to file and complete an application for permanent residence. To be successful, the immigrants had to show that they had been in the U.S. since being accepted in the

■ By the mid-1980s, the U.S. had opened its doors to immigrants from around the world. Immigration records show most legal immigrants came from Asia and Latin America. The number of immigrants who entered illegally is unknown.

1981	596,586
1982	594,131
1983	559,763
1984	543,903
1985	570,009
1986	601,708
1987	601,516
1988	643,000
1989/1990	1,289,384

program, had no criminal record, tested negative for HIV antibodies, were not on welfare, and had a knowledge of U.S. history and language. If this was not all completed in the time allotted, amnesty was withdrawn, and the person became an illegal alien subject to deportation. After being landed immigrants for five years, newcomers are able to apply for citizenship.

Naturalization Ceremony

On June 22, 1981, thousands of people took the oath that made them U.S. citizens. Ninety-seven thousand immigrants gathered at the same time in Memorial Stadium in Los Angeles to become nationals. It was the

■ Hopeful immigrants pledge allegiance to the flag in their bid for U.S. citizenship.

largest naturalization ceremony ever held in the U.S. The enormous swearing-in ceremony reflected the dramatic increase in immigration in the 1980s. Around 808,000 people, most of them from Asia and the Pacific Rim, arrived in the U.S. in 1980.

The Death of a Legend

John Lennon was a member of the British pop group, the Beatles, until the 1970s. After being in the spotlight for a decade, Lennon and his wife, Yoko Ono, withdrew from public life to raise their son. In 1980, Lennon was ready to reappear. He began granting interviews, and he and Ono produced their *Double Fantasy* album. It contained a number-one hit, "(Just Like) Starting Over." In an interview on December 5, Lennon looked forward to years of making music and helping bring about world peace. But he only had three more days to live. On December 8, he signed an autograph for a fan named Mark David Chapman. Hours later, Lennon returned to his New York apartment after a recording session. Chapman was still there waiting for him. He had been a fan of Lennon's but was now convinced that his hero had become a sellout. The obsessed fan shot Lennon dead on his doorstep. Lennon's death shocked and angered people around the world. The music legend, who had stood for peace and love, had been violently murdered. Thousands of mourners held non-stop **vigils** for their slain hero.

> "You know, give peace a chance, not shoot people for peace. All we need is love. I believe it.... I absolutely believe it."
>
> *John Lennon three days before his death*

RAPPING ALONG

■ Run-DMC introduced America to a new style of music called rap. At first, rap was performed mainly by inner-city African-American and Latino teenagers. In 1984, Run-DMC released its self-titled record, which was the first rap album to sell 500,000 copies. The group's music video was the first rap video played on MTV. Many other artists could relate to the message in the music and started rapping. Rap and hip-hop, a term for urban music, fashion, slang, and dance styles, spread like wildfire. Rap style included warm-up suits and baggy jeans, baseball caps turned backward or sideways, and expensive running shoes. Rap also became a way for people to protest violence, poverty, and racism in the U.S.

Moonwalker Dancing on Air

Michael Jackson fans were thrilled with his 1982 album. With smash hits, such as "Thriller," "Billy Jean," and "Beat It," *Thriller* quickly shot to the top. It stayed there for thirty-seven weeks. The album found its way into the *Guinness Book of World Records* as the best-selling album in history. By 1984, *Thriller* had sold 30 million copies worldwide. Jackson took advantage of the new 24-hour music video station. He released a fourteen-minute video of "Thriller." In it, he turns into a werewolf, terrorizes his girlfriend, and dances with zombies. Jackson produced top-quality videos and songs throughout the 1980s, and he earned the nickname "The King of Pop." At the 1984 Grammy Awards, Jackson was nominated for twelve awards and went home with eight—more Grammies than anyone had ever won at the awards ceremony. His 1987 album, *Bad*, was very successful as well, boasting five number-one hits.

■ Michael Jackson is known for his trendsetting style. Red leather jackets and single white gloves were hot items in the '80s.

Live Aid

A severe drought in the 1980s left millions of people starving in Africa. Music stars were not about to sit around and do nothing. In 1984, Bob Geldof, an Irish musician, arranged for a group of musicians to record a song to help raise money for aid in Africa. "Do They Know It's Christmas" earned millions of dollars for famine relief. The next year, on July 13, Geldof helped organize a huge concert to raise more money for famine victims. Sixty top artists performed for free at two enormous outdoor concerts—one in London and the other in Philadelphia. Madonna, U2, Queen, Tina Turner, Dire Straits, and other superstars performed for seventeen minutes each, and viewers were asked to phone in donations. More than 160,000 fans watched the shows in person, and another 1.5 billion watched on television. The concerts were called Live Aid, and viewers pledged $50 million to help ease the pain of famine.

MADONNA

■ Madonna arrived in New York in 1978 with $37 in her pocket and a dream of becoming a star. Four years later, she got her chance. She released her first pop dance single, "Everybody." Her success, some say, is due to MTV. Her music was good, but it was not enough to set her apart. It was her expertly crafted music videos that drew attention to her, along with her sassy looks, complicated dance moves, and unique style. Her debut album, *Madonna*, sold 3 million copies. Her single "Like a Virgin" was number one for six weeks in 1984. Madonna released six records during the decade. By the end of the 1980s, Madonna had turned her $37 into more than $100 million. Madonna has continued to release albums into the 21st century.

■ Live Aid drew one of the largest television audiences in history.

Bruce Springsteen

In 1984, people around the world knew where Springsteen came from. His album, *Born in the USA*, was the best-selling record of the year in England and America. It sold about 13 million copies worldwide and earned him a Grammy Award in 1985 for best rock vocalist. Springsteen sang about blue-collar America, and fans understood. Springsteen had all-American appeal. The release and success of *Born in the USA* launched him into a world concert tour. He put on a fantastic show for his audiences. His next wildly successful album, *Tunnel of Love* (1987), led to another Grammy Award and another world tour. This six-week tour raised money for Amnesty International. Springsteen had become one of the biggest rock and roll stars in the world.

Free Trade

In 1986, Canadian Prime Minister Brian Mulroney and President Reagan began working on a trade agreement that would make it easier to buy and sell goods over the border. The leaders agreed to remove **tariffs** on goods crossing the border by 1998. They also agreed to take away investment restrictions that were in place. Canada and the U.S. were strong trade partners, and the deal would mean a boost to both countries' economies. Despite some initial debate, the agreement was signed. It paved the way for the North American Free Trade Agreement (NAFTA), which added Mexico to the agreement in 1994.

GRENADA INVASION

■ The Caribbean island of Grenada became independent in 1974. Only five years later, the first prime minister was overthrown by Maurice Bishop. A second coup, and the murder of Bishop, occurred in 1983. There was great concern about the Marxist rebels that had taken power. On October 25, President Reagan and members of the Organization of East Caribbean States sent combat troops into the area. The troops remained there until the end of the year. An interim government was established in 1984, and fair elections were held. The invasion was viewed as a success in the U.S., but it was criticized by much of the rest of the world.

■ Ronald Reagan speaks with Brian Mulroney at the Quebec City Shamrock Summit on St. Patrick's Day, 1985.

Rocky Relationship

In the 1980s, relations between Libya and the U.S. were strained. President Reagan thought that Libya's leader, Colonel Muammar al-Qadhafi, supported terrorists. The Libyan leader felt that the U.S. was trying to **undermine** his government. In 1981, Reagan increased U.S. military presence in countries neighboring Libya. U.S. troops shot down two Libyan planes that were attacking U.S. pilots. U.S. sources believe that al-Qadhafi tried to kill U.S. diplomats and planned to kill Reagan in retaliation.

U.S. companies such as Exxon Oil withdrew from Libya. Reagan encouraged other U.S. businesses to leave, too. In March 1982, the government announced a boycott of Libyan oil. The loss of money caused problems for Libya. It pulled its forces out of Chad, where it had been supporting a civil war. This was the beginning of a rocky relationship between the U.S. and Libya.

Conflict With Lebanon

On June 6, 1982, Israeli forces invaded and occupied Lebanon in an attempt to bring an end to the Palestine Liberation Organization (PLO), which had been responsible for the deaths of many Israelis. During the occupation, pro-Israeli militias invaded Palestinian refugee camps and killed thousands of refugees. As well, many Lebanese civilians were killed by Israeli bombs in Lebanon's capital city, Beirut.

International peacekeepers were unable to ease the conflict. It continued until 1985 when Israeli troops withdrew from some of the territory they had occupied. Israeli forces did not withdraw completely from Lebanon until 2000.

■ A Palestinian child plays in the remains of his refugee camp home. Bombshells and destroyed vehicles take the place of dolls and bicycles.

American Invasion

In December 1989, President Bush sent troops into the Central American country of Panama. He wanted General Manuel Noriega arrested for drug trafficking. He also wanted to defend the 35,000 Americans who were living in Panama and defending the Panama Canal. Once Noriega was overthrown, Bush was friendly with the new leader, President Guillermo Endara. In 1990, Noriega turned himself in to U.S. officials and went to the U.S. to stand trial. He was convicted of drug trafficking in 1992 and sentenced to forty years in prison.

COMRADES WITH RUSSIA

■ President Bush kept up the good relations with the USSR that Ronald Reagan had begun. In 1989, Bush and USSR President Mikhail Gorbachev met on a Soviet ship near the coast of Malta. The two leaders discussed the rapid changes that were happening in Europe. While they did not come to any formal agreements, both sides acknowledged the importance of cooperation. The following year, the leaders met in the U.S. Both agreed to destroy their chemical weapons in the name of world peace. Throughout his term as president, George Bush continued to encourage economic relationships with the USSR.

American Events of the 1980s

Which of the following events happened in the eighties?

1
a) The movie *Star Wars* was released.
b) There was a nuclear attack by the USSR.
c) A defense plan called "Star Wars" was proposed by President Reagan.

2
a) Canada, Mexico, and the U.S. set up trade restrictions.
b) The U.S. and Mexico eliminated trade tariffs.
c) Canada and the U.S. eliminated trade tariffs.

3
a) The ERA amendment was three states short of passing.
b) President Reagan blocked the ERA from passing.
c) The ERA was passed unanimously by all legislatures.

5
a) Michael Jackson won eight Grammy Awards for *Thriller*.
b) Michael Jackson released "Man in the Mirror."
c) Michael Jackson married Lisa Marie Presley.

4
a) NASA launched *Voyager 1* space probe.
b) NASA's probe *Voyager 2* sent back photos of Neptune.
c) NASA launched *Voyager 1* and *2*.

1. c); 2 c); 3 a); 4 b); 5 a).

Choose the right answer:

1. Mount Saint Helens was in the news because
a) it was climbed for the first time in 1986.
b) it was the site for Steven Spielberg's movie, *E.T.*
c) it was a volcano that erupted.
d) the prime minister of Israel's plane crashed into it.

2. *Miami Vice* was
a) a law enforcement organization.
b) an instrument used in carpentry to keep pieces of wood secure.
c) a singing group.
d) a fashion-friendly television show.

3. Sandra Day O'Connor became
a) the first woman in space.
b) the first female Supreme Court judge.
c) an Olympic gymnast.
d) president of Chrysler.

4. Moonwalking was
a) a dance move.
b) the first steps on the moon
c) a part of "Star Wars."
d) discovered by *Voyager 2*.

Answers: 1 c); 2 d); 3 b); 4 a).

True or False

1. John Lennon was killed in a random shooting.

2. Christa McAuliffe was the first private citizen on a space shuttle flight.

3. Kareem Abdul-Jabbar scored 38,387 career points in professional basketball.

4. Fifty-seven hostages were taken by Iranians.

5. Salman Rushdie hid from Islamic terrorists after releasing *The Satanic Verses*.

Answers:
1. F (He was killed by an obsessed fan)
2. T
3. T
4. F (There were fifty-two hostages)
5. F (He hid from Islamic religious fundamentalists).

Newsmakers

Match the person or people in the news with their story!

1. caught as a spy

2. created company to produce virtual reality

3. won the Tour de France

4. science fiction writer

5. organized Live Aid

6. played Indiana Jones

7. Polish Solidarity leader

8. tried to assassinate President Reagan

9. president of Chrysler

10. designed the Vietnam Memorial

a) Bob Geldof
b) Lech Walesa
c) John Hinkley, Jr.
d) Jaron Lanier
e) Lee Iacocca
f) Maya Yang Lin
g) John Walker, Jr.
h) Greg LeMond
i) Harrison Ford
j) William Gibson

Answers: 1 g); 2 d); 3 h); 4 j); 5 a); 6 i); 7 b); 8 c); 9 e); 10 f).

alien: a foreign-born resident

amnesty: a pardon for past offences against a government

antitrust: the law against one company controlling an industry

appellate: the court that reviews the decisions of lower courts

bounty: a reward or payment given in return for a service

boycott: to show disapproval by refusing to have dealings with an organization or government

Cold War: the tension between the U.S. and the Soviet Union from the 1950s until the 1980s. There was not a official war, but there was distrust and rivalry between the two countries.

compatriots: people from the same country

consolidated: combined to make stronger

derogatory: showing an unfavorable opinion of someone or something

ecological: to do with the relationship of living things and their environment

espionage: spying

forbade: was not allowed

fundamentalists: people with strict religious beliefs

grueling: very tiring

inauguration: the ceremony that admits a person to public office

inducted: formal installation

martial law: military rule imposed on people. It overrides ordinary rules and laws.

poverty line: the minimum income needed to buy the basic necessities of life

quashed: crushed or rejected

sanctions: actions taken to penalize a country for human rights violations or to convince it to change its practices

serials: a story presented in parts

stalemate: a deadlock with no clear winner

tariffs: fees or taxes added to imports and exports.

undermine: to weaken gradually

vigils: a night spent in prayer or mourning

Zionist: supporter of a worldwide Jewish movement that promotes the state of Israel as a homeland for Jews

Learning More

Here are some book resources and Internet links if you want to learn more about the people, places, and events that made headlines during the 1980s.

Books

Berger, Gilda. *USA for Africa: Rock Aid in the Eighties*. New York: Franklin Watts, 1987.

Brewster, Todd, and Peter Jennings. *The Century for Young People*. New York: Random House, 1999.

Clifton, Daniel, ed. *Chronicle of America*. New York: Dorling Kindersley, 1997.

Duden, Jane, and Gail B. Stewart. *1980s*. Timelines series. New York: Macmillan, Crestwood House, 1991.

Rettemund, Matthew. *Totally Awesome Eighties*. New York: St. Martin's Press, 1996.

Tames, Richard. *The 1980s*. Picture History of the 20th Century series. New York: Franklin Watts, 1990.

Internet Links

http://cbs.infoplease.com/encyclopdict.html

http://arc.iki.rssi.ru/solar/eng/history.htm

http://www.nasa.gov/kids.html

For information about other U.S. subjects, type your key words into a search engine such as Alta Vista or Yahoo!

USA 1980s Index

Abdul-Jabbar, Kareem 30, 45
Academy Award 11
AIDS 5, 6, 27
aliens 38, 39, 46
animation 10
arcades 13
artificial heart 27
assassinations 22
AT&T 35

Berlin Wall 4, 5, 7, 18, 44
Bhopal 7, 18
Bishop, Maurice 42
Black Monday 5, 7, 34
Blume, Judy 25
boycott 7, 28, 42, 46
Brat Pack 10
break dancing 15
Bush, George 7, 20, 23, 43

Cabbage Patch Kids 14
Castro, Fidel 6, 38
CDs 14
Challenger 4, 7, 8, 26
Chernobyl 4, 7, 16
Chrysler 35, 45
CNN 12
Cold War 20, 22, 46
computers 26
Cuba 38

earthquake 4, 9
Equal Rights Amendment (ERA) 6, 33, 44
espionage 23, 46
E.T. 4, 11, 44
Exxon *Valdez* 8

famine 4, 5, 7, 17, 41
Ferraro, Geraldine 21
fitness 15, 37
Fonda, Jane 15
Ford, Harrison 11, 45
Fox, Michael J. 11

Gibson, William 24, 45
glasnost 19
Gorbachev, Mikhail 7, 19, 20, 43

homelessness 33
hostages 19, 20, 21, 45

Iran 7, 19, 20, 21, 25
Iran Contra 21
Iraq 7, 19, 20, 23

Jackson, Michael 36, 40, 44
Joyner, Florence Griffith 4, 29

Khomeini, Ayatollah 20, 25
King, Stephen 25

Lebanon 4, 22, 43
LeMond, Greg 29, 45
Lennon, John 40, 45
Lewis, Carl 4, 28
Libya 8, 42
Live Aid 5, 7, 41, 45

Madonna 36, 41
M*A*S*H 6, 13
McAuliffe, Christa 8, 45
Miami Vice 37, 44
Mount Saint Helens 6, 9, 44
MTV 6, 10, 40, 41

NAFTA 42
NASA 8, 12, 26, 27, 44, 47
Navratilova, Martina 31
Nobel Prize 16, 18
Noriega, Manuel 23, 43

perestroika 19
Pollard, Jonathan 23
Pulitzer Prize 24

Reagan, Ronald 6, 8, 20, 21, 22, 23, 33, 34, 35, 42, 43, 44, 45
Ride, Sally 26
Rose, Pete 7, 31
Rubik, Erno 15
Run-DMC 40
Rushdie, Salman 7, 25, 45

Schwarzenegger, Arnold 13
smuggling 5, 38
solidarity 18, 45
Spencer, Diana 19
Spielberg, Steven 10, 11, 44
Springsteen, Bruce 41
"Star Wars" 22, 44
Supreme Court 33, 44
Swatch 14

Tan, Amy 24
terrorism 22
Tiananmen Square 7, 17
Tour de France 29, 45
Turner, Ted 12
Tyson, Mike 31

video games 13
Vietnam Memorial 6, 32, 45
virtual reality 24, 26, 45
Voyager 26, 44

Walker, Alice 24